Date: 7/9/18

J 324.6 GUN
Gunderson, Jessica,
Understanding your role in
elections /

Fact Finders®

Kids' Guide to Government

UNDERSTANDING YOUR ROLE IN ELECTIONS

by Jessica Gunderson

Consultant: Steven S. Smith, PhD
Professor of Political Science
Washington University

CAPSTONE PRESS
a capstone imprint

Fact Finders Books are published by Capstone Press,
1710 Roe Crest Drive, North Mankato, Minnesota 56003
www.mycapstone.com

Library of Congress Cataloging-in-Publication Data
Library of Congress Cataloging-in-Publication data is available on the Library
of Congress website.
ISBN 978-1-5435-0318-0 (library binding)
ISBN 978-1-5435-0322-7 (paperback)
ISBN 978-1-5435-0326-5 (eBook PDF)

Editorial Credits
Michelle Hasselius, editor; Mackenzie Lopez, designer;
Jo Miller, media researcher; Kathy McColley, production specialist

Image Credits
Dreamstime: Paul Simcock, 5; Getty Images: Bettmann, 18 (top), The Image
Bank/Dirk Anschutz, 29; Library of Congress, Prints and Photographs
Division, 17; Newscom: CQ Roll Call/Tom Williams, 9, Everett Collection,
19; Shutterstock: -Taurus-, 8, Aniwhite, 23, DNetromphotos, 24, Evan El-
Amin, 25, 27 (right), Everett Historical, 18 (bottom), 27 (left, middle left,
middle), Incomible, 11, Jonathan Weiss, 6, LANTERIA, 12, 26, Raksha Shelare,
cover, SAlexandru Nika, 21, Sashkin, 14 (button backgrounds), South12th
Photography, 22; Wikimedia: Green Party of the United States, 15, Libertarian
Party, 15, Republican National Committee, 14, United States Democratic Party,
14, White House photo by Eric Draper, 27 (middle right)

Design Credits
Capstone

Printed and bound in Canada.
010801S18

TABLE OF CONTENTS

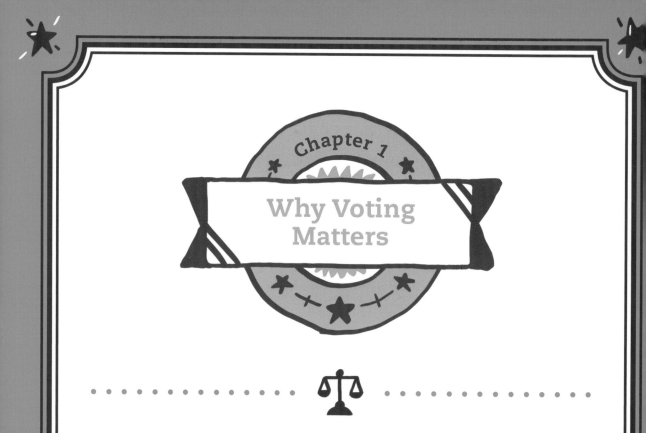

Chapter 1
Why Voting Matters

Imagine yourself on a typical school day. Are the roads paved on your ride to school? What is the speed limit? Is there a crosswalk in front of your school? When you get to class, what subjects will you learn about? What will you eat for lunch? At the end of the day, what time do you go home?

Surprisingly, the answers to all of these questions have to do with voting. When people vote, they elect officials to make decisions for the community.

Elected officials or **representatives** vote on laws, such as how fast or slow speed limits should be. They help decide how to spend the money collected from taxes. This money could be used to pave roads or add street signs near your school. Officials even help determine what subjects you will study and how long your school day will be. When people vote, they choose representatives who they think will make the right decisions for them. Voting matters!

representative—someone chosen to speak or act for others

The Three Branches of Government

The United States is a **democracy**. Citizens vote for officials to represent them on the local, state, and federal levels. The United States federal government has three parts that work together. These parts are called branches. The three branches of the federal government are the legislative branch, the executive branch, and the judicial branch. The legislative branch makes laws that govern the country, the executive branch carries out the laws, and the judicial branch makes sure the laws follow the U.S. Constitution.

Indiana State House of Representatives in 2017

democracy—country that has an elected government
population—total number of people who live in a place
appoint—choose someone for a job

LEGISLATIVE BRANCH

The legislative branch consists of the U.S. Congress. Members of Congress write and vote on laws. The U.S. Congress has two sections — the Senate and the House of Representatives. Each state has two senators. A state's number of representatives is based on the state's **population**. The higher a state's population, the more representatives that state has.

EXECUTIVE BRANCH

The executive branch is made up of the U.S. president and his or her cabinet. The president leads the country, commands our nation's military, and makes sure our laws are followed. The cabinet includes the vice president and cabinet members. The president chooses his or her cabinet members. The Senate must approve the selected cabinet members. Cabinet members give the president advice based on their areas of expertise. For example, the Secretary of Education advises the president on matters related to schools and education.

JUDICIAL BRANCH

The judicial branch consists of judges and the court system. Judges interpret the law and make sure it is being followed according to the U.S. Constitution. The highest court in the country is the Supreme Court. The Supreme Court has nine judges. The president **appoints** federal judges and Supreme Court justices. The Senate votes to approve the judges or justices that the president selects. Federal judges and Supreme Court justices hold their positions for life.

Which Branch Is the Strongest?

Which branch of government do you think is the strongest? The answer is none of them. Each branch keeps the balance of power.

To understand how this works, let's take a closer look at how a **bill** becomes law. Members of Congress vote on a bill they hope will become law. If the bill passes the Senate and the House of Representatives, it is sent to the president. The bill becomes law if the president signs it. The president can also **veto** the bill. If this happens, the bill goes back to Congress. If Congress has enough votes, it can overrule the president's veto and the bill comes law. Later, a judge could rule that the law is illegal if it doesn't follow the Constitution.

Who Can Run for Office?

Anyone can run for office in America. Well, almost anyone. To run for president, you have to be born in the United States. You must be at least 35 years old. You also must have lived in this country for at least 14 years.

To be a U.S. senator, you have to be a U.S. citizen for at least nine years. You must be at least 30 years old and live in the state you want to represent.

To be a U.S. representative, you must be a U.S. citizen for at least seven years. You have to be at least 25 years old and live in the state you want to represent.

Catherine Cortez Masto was sworn in as a senator for Nevada in 2003.

bill—written plan for a new law, to be debated in Congress
veto—reject a bill proposed by Congress

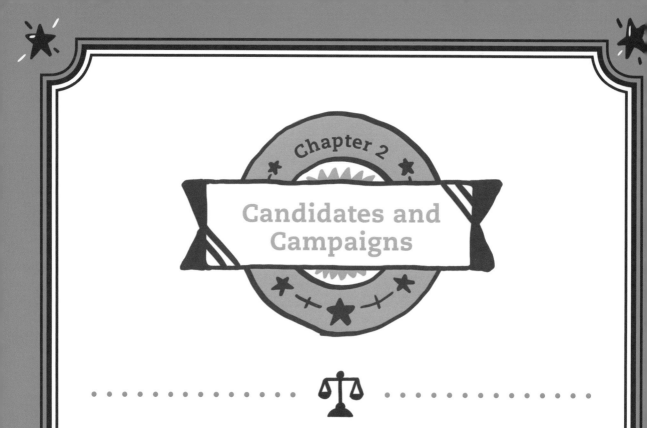

Chapter 2
Candidates and Campaigns

If you've watched TV during an election year, you've seen commercials about **candidates** running for office. These advertisements are part of a candidate's **campaign**. A campaign is a series of activities that encourage citizens to vote for a certain politician.

Candidates campaign in many different ways. Their supporters put advertisements on TV, radio, and social media. Volunteers distribute flyers, buttons, T-shirts, and bumper stickers.

Many candidates tour the state or country and hold **rallies**. During the rallies, candidates speak to crowds about what they will do if elected. Sometimes supporters speak at the rallies too. They tell the crowds why they support the candidate.

FACT

Candidates often have slogans. A slogan is a catchy phrase that sums up a candidate's goal. In the 2016 presidential election, Donald Trump's campaign slogan was "Make America Great Again!" Slogans are printed on hats, shirts, and buttons for supporters to wear.

candidate—someone who is applying for a job or trying to be elected to an office or post

campaign—series of activities organized to win an election

rally—large gathering of people with similar interests

Candidates also participate in **debates** with other candidates who are running for the same office. During most debates, a **moderator** asks the candidates specific questions about issues that voters feel are important. The candidates take turns answering the questions. They are usually given a set amount of time to answer. Debates help voters understand each candidate's plan and viewpoints. You may be able to attend the debates but most people watch them on TV or online.

Campaign Funding

Campaigns can be very expensive. A candidate may pay for some of his or her campaign. Citizens also donate money to candidates they believe in. Campaign funding also comes from political action committees, or PACs. PACs are created by political groups and large corporations. PACs donate money to candidates based on who they think will best serve their interests.

debate—discussion between sides with different views; candidates hold debates before elections
moderate—lead or preside over a meeting

13

Political Parties

Most candidates running for office represent political parties. A political party is a group that stands for certain ideas and policies. Before presidential elections, voters must choose from a list of candidates in the same party. In the summer of a presidential election year, major political parties hold national conventions. **Delegates** from each state attend the convention.

Democratic Party

formed in 1828

The nation's oldest active political party believes in a strong federal government, rules and laws for business, government-funded social programs to help the poor, and protection of the environment.

Republican Party

formed in 1854

Also called the Grand Old Party or GOP, this party believes in small federal government and strong state and local governments, strong military, and less government spending for social programs.

These delegates vote for their party's candidate. Delegates base their votes on the winner of the primary election for their state. The candidate chosen at the convention is the presidential **nominee** for that party.

delegate—someone who represents other people at a meeting
nominee—someone who is chosen to run in an election

Libertarian Party

formed in 1971
This party believes in personal freedoms, lowering taxes, and getting rid of many laws, such as drug and drinking age laws.

Green Party

formed in the 1990s
This party believes in protecting the environment, nonviolence, and is antiwar. It does not accept donations from corporations.

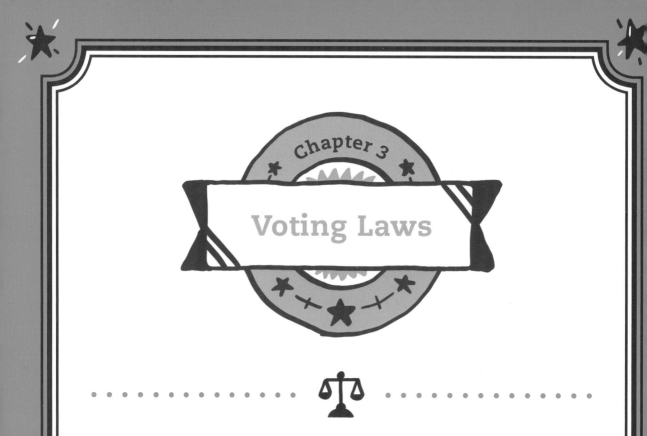

Chapter 3

Voting Laws

If you are at least 18 years old and a U.S. citizen, you can vote in U.S. elections. But this wasn't always the case.

When the United States was founded, only white males who owned land were allowed to vote. Eventually many states got rid of land requirements. By the mid-1800s all white male citizens could vote. However African-Americans, other **minorities,** and women could not. During this time women and minority groups didn't have the same rights as white men.

The 15th Amendment

The 15th Amendment was **ratified** in 1870, giving black men the right to vote. However, many states in the south passed laws to keep black Americans from voting. Some southern states required all voters to pay fees. Others also required voters to take tests to prove they could read and write. Many black voters could not afford the fees. Most former slaves could not read or write. Some black voters were also threatened or even killed if they tried to vote.

The Civil War

The Battle of Pea Ridge in 1862

In 1860 many people living in the south worried they would lose their rights to own slaves. By 1861, 11 southern states had **seceded** from the United States. The Civil War broke out between the northern and southern states in April 1861. In 1863 President Abraham Lincoln declared that all southern slaves were free. When the Civil War ended in 1865, slavery in America ended as well.

minority—group of people of a particular race, ethnic group, or religion living among a larger group of a different race, ethnic group, or religion

ratify—agree to or approve officially

secede—formally withdraw from a group or an organization, often to form another organization

The 19th Amendment

In the early 1900s, women fought for the right to vote in the United States. They wanted to have a say in what happened in their government. The fight for women's voting rights was called the Suffrage Movement. In 1920 the 19th Amendment was ratified, giving women the right to vote. Over time women started running for office.

Victoria Woodhull in 1872

FACT

In 1872 Victoria Woodhull became the first woman to run for president, almost 50 years before women won the right to vote. That means Woodhull couldn't even vote for herself!

Women suffragists put up a billboard advertising their parade for voting rights in 1914

Voting Rights Act of 1965

In the 1960s black citizens fought for equality during the Civil Rights Movement. When the Voting Rights Act was passed in 1965, it outlawed voter **discrimination**. States were no longer allowed to make laws that could prevent minorities from voting. Literacy tests could not be given to voters. The Voting Rights Act also made it illegal for individuals to threaten or keep people from voting.

Black protesters marched in Washington, D.C., in the 1960s.

FACT

In 1895 seven southern states passed the grandfather clause. This clause stated that you could vote without paying a fee if your grandfather voted prior to 1866. This excluded black Americans because their grandfathers were usually slaves and couldn't vote.

discrimination—prejudice or unfair behavior toward others based on differences such as age, race, and gender

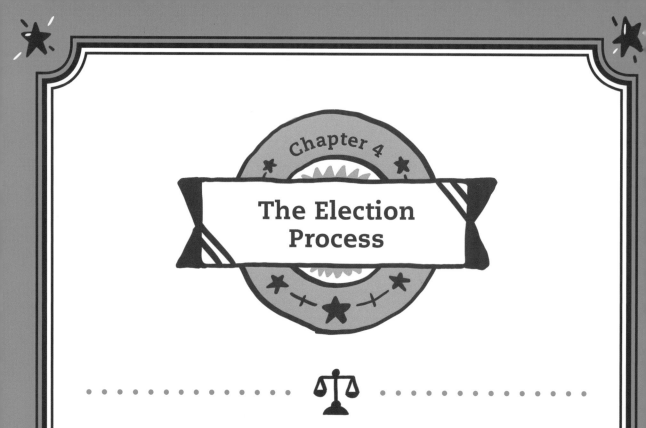

Chapter 4

The Election Process

Elections for the U.S. Senate and the House of Representatives are held every two years in November. A presidential election is held every four years. The elections held on non-presidential years are called midterm elections.

The voting process in general elections differs from state to state. Voters have to register to vote in the state in which they live. They must provide information about who they are, such as when they were born and where they live. In some states a voter must also show a photo ID before voting.

On Election Day, voters go to polling places to cast their vote. Polling places are usually set up in public buildings, such as schools and post offices. Voters are assigned polling places based on where they live. According to voting laws, a citizen can only vote once. If someone tries to vote more than once, it is called voter fraud. The person could be arrested.

What's a Ballot?

Citizens cast their votes on **ballots**. The names of the candidates are on the ballot. There could be candidates running for president, U.S. senator, U.S. representative, state governor, state senator, and state representative. There may also be local candidates running for mayor, city council, or school board. Sometimes there are also **referendums** on the ballot. A referendum is a suggested law. For example, there might be a referendum asking if voters want to raise taxes to fund schools.

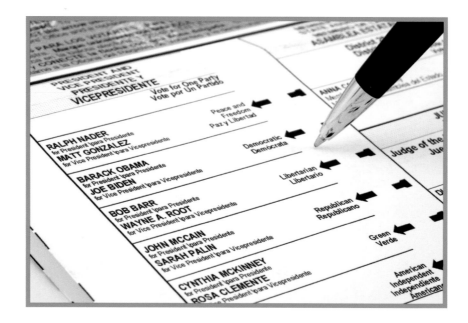

ballot—secret way of voting, such as on a machine or on a slip of paper
referendum—a vote by the people on a public measure

Ballots differ from state to state. Some ballots are electronic. Voters use voting machines or computers to mark their choices. Other states use paper ballots. Voters cast their votes by filling in circles on the ballot. Then they drop the ballots into a ballot box.

The Electoral College

After the polls close, votes are counted. Usually the candidate with the most votes wins. But the process to elect our nation's president is different. We use a process called the Electoral College. During the presidential election, voters make their choice for the president. This vote is called the popular vote. But voters aren't voting for the president directly. Instead, they are voting for a group of electors from a political party. The electors will then officially choose the president later.

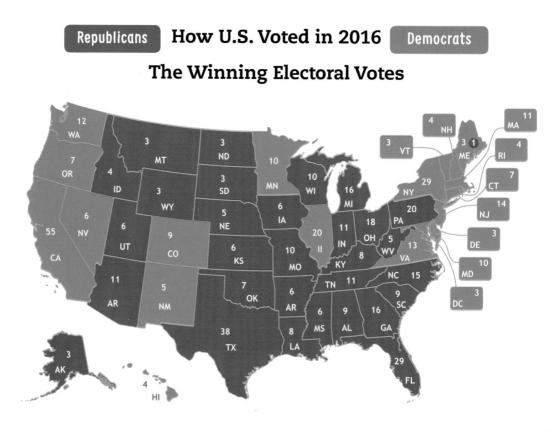

| Republicans | **How U.S. Voted in 2016** | Democrats |

The Winning Electoral Votes

Each state gets a certain number of electors. The number is based on how many senators and representatives the state has in Congress. Electors pledge to vote for the presidential candidate who receives the majority of the votes in their state. For example, the majority of the voters in Massachusetts voted for Hillary Clinton in the 2016 presidential election. In this "winner-take-all" system, Massachusetts' 11 electoral votes went to the Democratic nominee. The candidate with the most votes usually gets all of the state's electoral votes.

Presidential candidate Hillary Clinton campaigned with Senator Elizabeth Warren at the Museum Center in Massachusetts.

FACT

Maine and Nebraska are the only two states that do not follow the "winner-take-all" system. These states are divided into districts, with one electoral vote for each district. This means the electoral votes for these states can be split between the presidential candidates.

Who Wins?

The electors cast the official vote for the president of the United States in December. There are currently a total of 538 electoral votes. The presidential nominee needs 270 electoral votes to win. It's possible that no candidate will reach 270 votes. If that happens, the U.S. House of Representatives will choose the winner.

Our nation's founders put the Electoral College process in place to balance the interests of small and large states. The founders also feared that the voters might choose a person who was unfit for the role.

Presidents Who Lost the Popular Vote

It is possible for a president to win the Electoral College but lose the popular vote. This has happened to five presidents so far: John Quincy Adams, Rutherford B. Hayes, Benjamin Harrison, George W. Bush, and Donald Trump.

John Quincy Adams   **Rutherford B. Hayes**   **Benjamin Harrison**   **George W. Bush**   **Donald Trump**

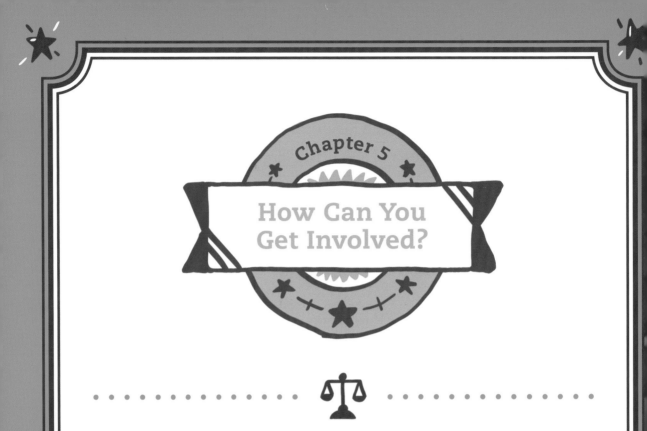

Chapter 5

How Can You Get Involved?

You may not be old enough to vote yet, but you can still get involved during election season. You can help distribute flyers and hang posters. You can wear T-shirts of your favorite candidates. You can watch debates to learn about each person's goals and beliefs.

Talk to your teacher about holding an election in class. You could campaign and vote for your favorite candidate. You could also vote for class officers, such as class president and class secretary. You could even run for these offices yourself.

Running for a class office can teach you about the roles our leaders play in society. You may even decide to pursue a career in politics. You could run for president one day!

Why Some People Don't Vote

In the 2016 presidential election, only about half of eligible voters cast their vote. That means more than 100 million Americans didn't vote!

People have different reasons for not voting. Some think their vote doesn't matter. Others might not like the candidates. Whatever the reason, the right to vote should not be taken for granted. People have fought hard to give Americans equal voting rights. Remember that you can make a difference. Every vote counts!

Glossary

appoint (uh-POINT)—choose someone for a job

ballot (BAL-uht)—secret way of voting, such as on a machine or on a slip of paper

bill (BIL)—written plan for a new law, to be debated in Congress

campaign (kam-PAYN)—series of activities organized to win an election

candidate (KAN-duh-date)—someone who is applying for a job or trying to be elected to an office or post

debate (di-BATE)—discussion between sides with different views

delegate (DEL-uh-gate)—someone who represents other people at a meeting

democracy (di-MOK-ruh-see)—country that has an elected government

discrimination (diss-krim-i-NAY-shuhn)—prejudice or unfair behavior to others based on differences such as age, race, and gender

minority (mye-NOR-uh-tee)—group of people of a particular race, ethnic group, or religion living among a larger group of a different race, ethnic group, or religion

moderate (MOD-uh-rate)—lead or preside over a meeting

nominee (nom-uh-NEE)—someone who is chosen to run in an election

population (pop-yuh-LAY-shun)—total number of people who live in a place

rally (RAL-ee)—large gathering of people with similar interests

ratify (RAT-uh-fye)—agree to or approve officially

representative (rep-ri-ZEN-tuh-tiv)—someone chosen to speak or act for others

referendum (rehf-er-EHN-duhm)—a vote by the people on a public measure

secede (si-SEED)—formally withdraw from a group or an organization, often to form another organization

veto (VEE-toh)—reject a bill proposed by Congress

Critical Thinking Questions

1. Describe the three branches of government and what each branch does.

2. A slogan is a phrase used by a business, group, or person to express a goal or belief. Think of a slogan you've heard recently on the radio or TV. What was it? What was the slogan for?

3. Only about half of eligible voters cast their vote in the last presidential election. What are some reasons why a person would choose not to vote? Use the text to help you with your answer.

Read More

Hajeski, Nancy J. *The Big Book of Presidents: From George Washington to Barack Obama.* New York: Skyhorse Publishing, Inc., 2015.

Krasner, Barbara. *A Timeline of Presidential Elections.* Presidential Politics. North Mankato, Minn.: Capstone Press, 2016

Sobel, Syl. *Presidential Elections and Other Cool Facts.* Hauppauge, N.Y.: Barron's, 2016.

Internet Sites

Use FactHound to find Internet sites related to this book.

Visit *www.facthound.com*.

Just type in 9781543503180 and go.

Check out projects, games and lots more at
www.capstonekids.com

Index